25 Crafts for a Rainy Day

Crafts by Christina Goodings
Photography by John Williams
Illustrated by Samantha Meredith

Contents

LION
CHILDREN'S

1 Gingerbread ark

God told Noah to build an ark big enough for him and his family, and two of every kind of animal.

Make your own Noah and Mrs Noah – and your own ark out of gingerbread!

1 Mix together in a bowl:
300g plain flour
1 teaspoon baking soda
1 teaspoon cinnamon
1 teaspoon ginger

2 Ask a grown-up to melt together in a saucepan:
125g butter
100g brown sugar
2 tablespoons black treacle

Pour the melted stuff into the bowl.
Stir to make a lump.
Chill in the fridge.

3 Roll out the lump on a piece of baking paper. Cut an ark shape like the one on the right and use a cookie cutter for Noah and his wife. Pull away the rest of the dough and lift the shapes with the paper onto an oven tray. Bake for about 10 minutes at 160°C. Leave to cool.

4 Decorate the gingerbread pieces with icing and sweets.

Make as many characters out of the dough as you can.

Have fun decorating your gingerbread as shown, or any way you like!

2 Walking animals

The animals followed Noah onto the ark two by two. By moving the sticks of these puppets, you can make them look like they're walking.

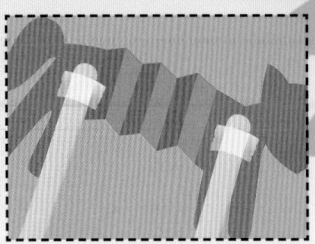

1 Practise drawing animals on scrap paper like the ones here, with long bodies and four legs.

2 Make zigzag folds along the middle so that the creature can jiggle. Adjust the design if needed. When you have got the shape right, cut it out.

3 Use this template to cut out the animal in your choice of card. Add features. These can be cut-out shapes you glue on or details you draw in marker or crayon.

4 Zigzag fold your creature. Then tape craft sticks on the wrong side by the front and back pairs of legs.

3 Happy frogs

Once everyone was safely on board, it started to rain. Frogs love rain – they must have been happy! Make your own.

 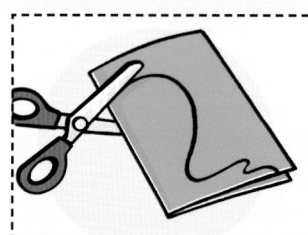  

1 Cut a square of green paper about 18cm x 10cm. Curl into a tube and tape in place.

2 Use the template at the back of this book to help draw the leg shape along the fold of a folded piece of green paper. Cut it out and glue on the back of the tube.

3 Cut white circles for eyes and draw in the centre of the eyes. Glue these on as shown. Add other details as you wish.

You can use the template at the back of this book to cut a lily pad for your frog to sit on!

4 Rain all around

It rained for forty days. The flood waters rose until they covered all the land.

Colour in this picture of the animals on the ark. How many pairs of animals can you find?

Tip – use bright felt tips on this paper or copy this page and use crayons and paints if you wish.

5 Finger puppets

The animals waited for the rain to stop. See how many different types of animals you can make as finger puppets.

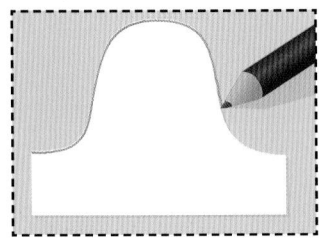

1 Copy the template for the basic finger puppet from the back of this book. Change the template size to suit your fingers. Cut it out on plain paper.

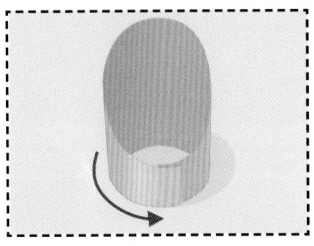

2 Fold back the sides and tape together. Check that you like the fit.

3 Cut more basic shapes this size for the animals. Cut out features in paper and glue them on. Add details in paints, crayons, or markers before taping to your finger.

6 Rainy day treats

Noah took on board enough food for his family and all the animals. Here are some sweet cookie treats for you to bake.

  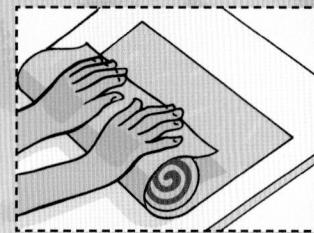 

1 Measure into a bowl 150g softened butter, 100g soft brown sugar, and 75g caster sugar. Mix together until light and creamy. Then ask a grown-up to help you add and mix in two eggs, one at a time. Add a spoonful of flour if needed.

2 Now divide the mix into two bowls. Sift into one bowl 175g self-raising flour and 1 teaspoon of vanilla essence. Mix well to make a dough. Sift into the other bowl 150g self-raising flour and 1 tablespoon of cocoa. Mix to make a dough.

3 Place baking parchment on your work surface. Roll out the vanilla dough to a rectangle about 30cm x 15cm and 3mm thick. Do the same with the chocolate dough. Slide the chocolate dough onto the vanilla dough and roll up together. Wrap in the parchment and chill overnight in the fridge.

4 When you are ready to bake the cookies, ask a grown-up to heat the oven to 180°C. Line a baking tray with parchment. Unwrap your dough and slice into cookies about 5mm thick. Bake for 8 minutes. Ask a grown-up to lift the tray out of the oven and leave the cookies to cool.

7 Searching dove

Eventually the rain stopped. The water went down and the ark got stuck on a mountaintop. Noah sent out a dove to look for land. It brought back an olive twig.

1 Take a sheet of paper 40cm x 40cm. Fold in half and half again.

2 Lay the folded paper with the fold to the left and top. Draw the wing and tail shape as shown (or copy the template at the back of this book). Cut out through all the layers. Decorate.

3 Draw a bird body on card (there is a template to copy at the back of this book). Cut it out and draw on the features.

4 Fold each side of the wing piece up as shown by the line here.

5 Spread glue along the top edge of the body and insert into the wings.

Add a thread so your bird can fly!

8 Rainbow colours

After the earth dried out, God put a rainbow in the sky as a sign of his promise never to flood the world again.

There are seven colours of the rainbow. Can you make some of them from the other colours with your paints?

red
orange
yellow
green
blue
indigo
violet

red + yellow   = orange

yellow + blue   = green

blue + red   = violet

9 Celebration flags

God told Noah to let all the animals go free again so that they could spread out all over the earth once more. Noah and his family celebrated. Here are some flags you can make to decorate a room for your own celebrations.

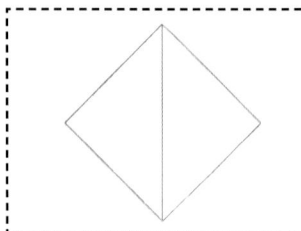

1 Take a square of paper (a good size is 15cm x 15cm) and lightly rule a diagonal line on the wrong side. Arrange the paper diamond-wise in front of you.

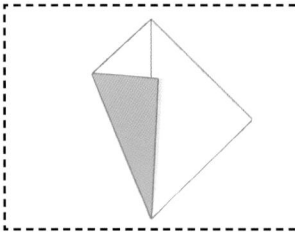

2 Now fold the left side so its top corner goes about 5mm over the centre line and its lower corner forms a point. Crease.

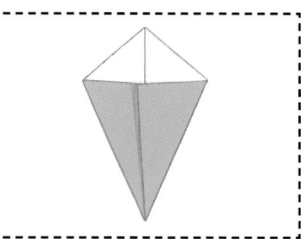

3 Fold and crease the right side in the same way. (If you want to put a treat in each flag, tape the edges to make a pocket.)

4 Next fold the top part
down. Fasten with a
sticker.

5 Decorate the front
side. Now punch a hole
at the top and thread
ribbon through. Tie
this in a bow onto your
hanging yarn.

10 Lion masks

Some of the animals on the ark were fierce and dangerous. Does being cooped up inside on a rainy day make you feel like a wild animal? By wearing this lion mask, you can pretend to be one!

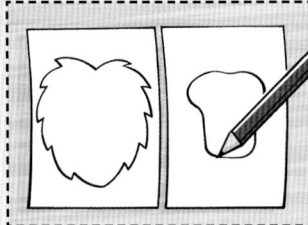

1 Trace or copy the outline of the mane and of the face at the back of this book onto thin white card. Cut out both shapes.

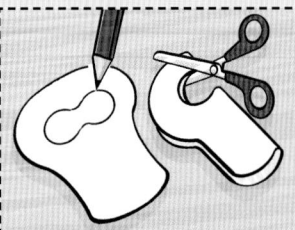

2 Beginning with the face, curl the shape in half lengthways and pinch the bit by the bridge of the nose so you can cut out the eye holes. Cut these out carefully and keep the eye piece.

3 Now put the face on the mane piece, and draw around the eye-shaped hole and cut out.

4 Paint the face and one pair of eye pieces in tawny yellow and the mane in tawny brown. Leave to dry.

5 Check the fit of the pieces on your face and mark small holes for elastic as shown. Punch the holes before you glue the shapes together.

6 Tear the painted eyepiece in two to make ears. Attach to your lion mask, as shown. Add details in marker. Finally tie the elastic through the holes at each side.

11 Roaming reptiles

Some of the animals who left the ark roamed over rocks and back into the rivers and seas – like crocodiles, alligators, and lizards. Make some of each!

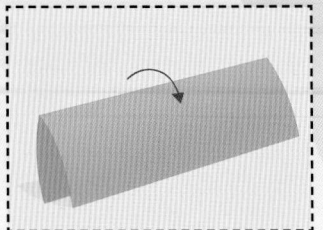

1 Cut a rectangle of paper about three times as long as it is wide (for example, 5cm x 15cm). Fold it in half lengthways and crease.

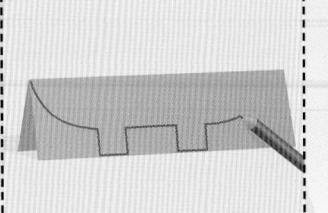

2 Rule a faint line about halfway up the folded rectangle. This marks the base of the body. Now mark the head, tail, and legs. Cut out the shape.

3 Now make diagonal snips along the back.

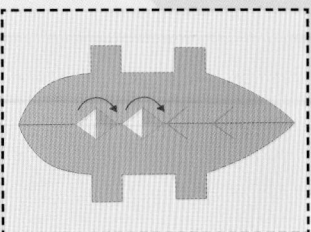

4 Open up the folded paper so you can fold the triangles made by the slits toward the tail. Refold the paper.

5 Finally, fold under 1cm on each of the legs to make feet, and use markers and cut-out shapes that you glue on to make the features.

12 Beautiful butterflies

Some of the animals flew back into the air. Butterflies come in all kinds of colours and patterns. Can you make butterflies as beautiful as real ones?

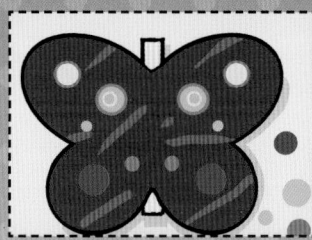

1 Choose thin card for the wings, almost as tall as a craft peg and twice as wide as its height. Fold it in half and draw a wing shape. Cut it out.

2 Unfold the wings and decorate with punched or cut-out paper shapes. Glue the wings to the peg.

3 Draw a body shape about the same size as your peg and cut it out. Add features with crayons or markers. Glue this on top of the wings.

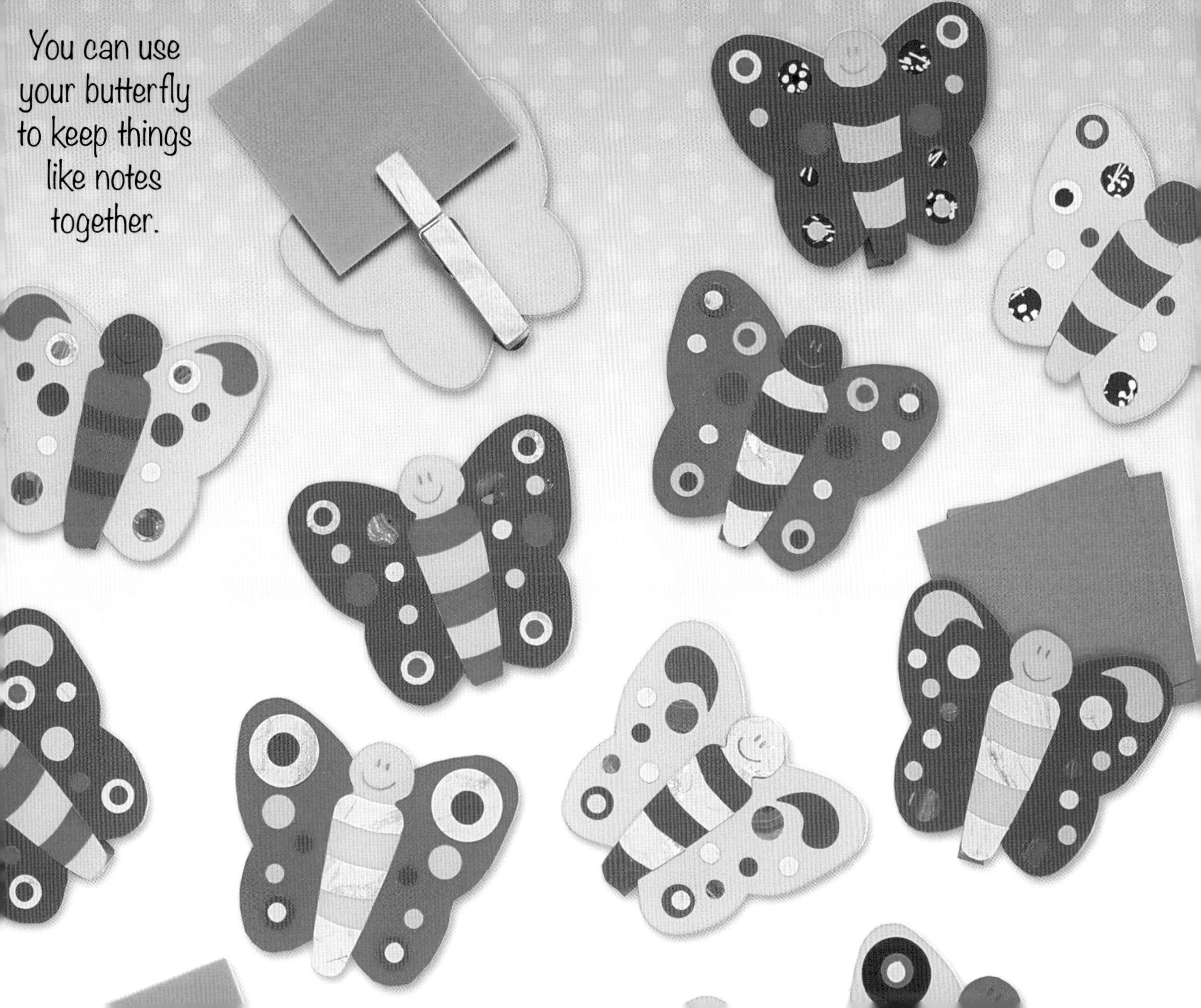

You can use your butterfly to keep things like notes together.

13 Family ties

As the years went by, Noah's sons and their wives had children, and their children had children. Their family grew and grew, and people journeyed to all parts of the earth.

Colour in this picture of families.

Tip - use bright felt tips on this paper or copy this page and use crayons and paints if you wish.

14 Cute bunnies

Some of the new baby animals were just too cute. These sweet bunnies are easy to make – so you can make lots!

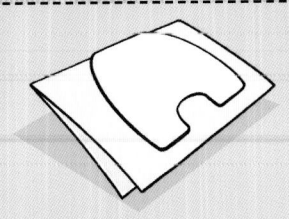

1 Copy the body and head shapes from the back of this book onto plain card. Cut them out to use as templates.

2 Fold a piece of pastel card for the body and line up the template with the fold. Draw and cut out the body.

3 Draw around the head piece on a single piece of pastel card. Cut out. If you wish, cut inner ears in white paper and glue them on.

4 Draw the face with markers and then glue the head in place on the body. Add details if you wish.

15 Tree cards

After the flood waters went away, the earth started to grow green again with new plants and trees. Make some tree cards.

1 Measure a square of card for the background. Fold it in half.

2 Now cut a strip of patterned paper for the top and bottom of the card and an oval for the tree. Glue these to the card as shown.

3 Cut a thin triangle to be the tree trunk and glue this on top.

4 Now choose butterflies, birds, flowers, and blossom stickers, or cut-out shapes. Glue them on to make your garden full of new spring life.

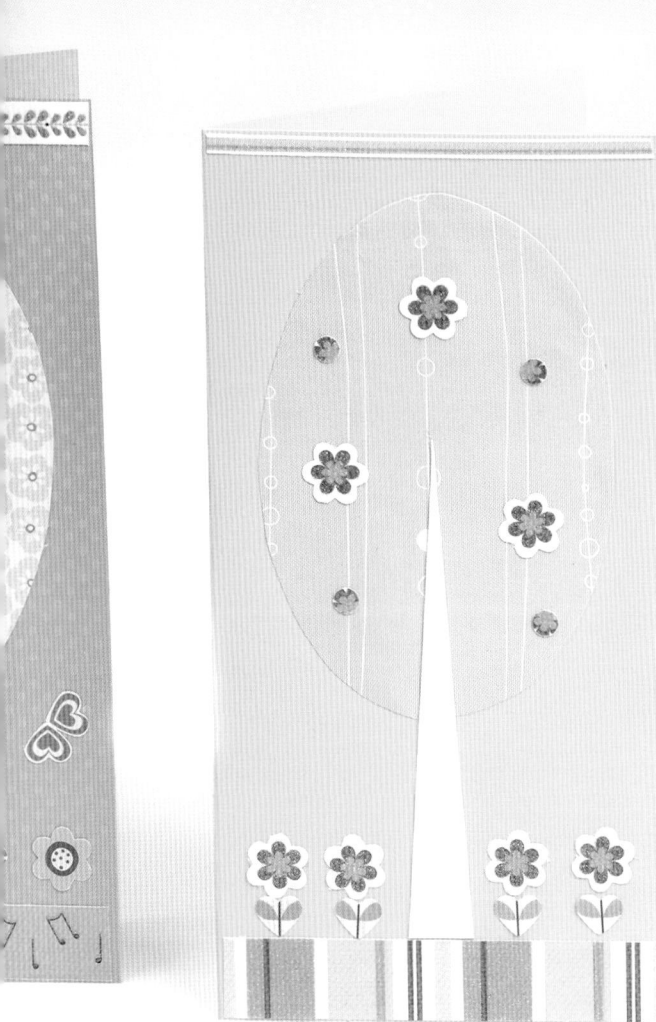

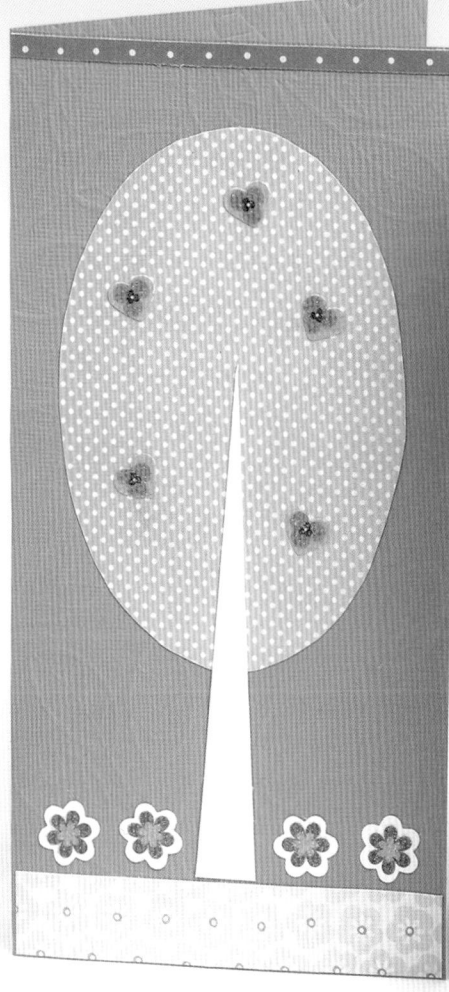

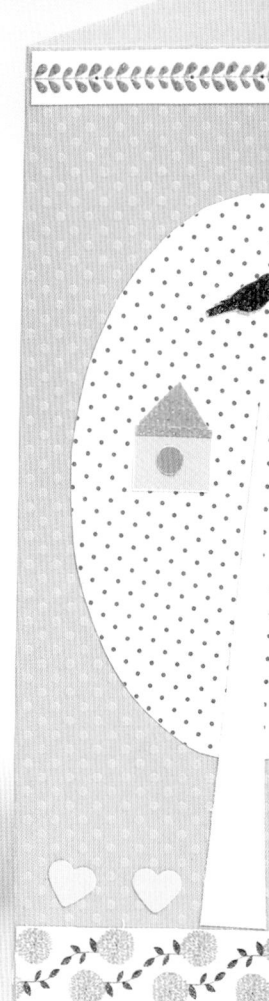

16 Papier mâché pals

God sent the flood as he thought that the people were becoming too careless. We need to look after our earth and its resources. This papier mâché craft recycles non-glossy paper.

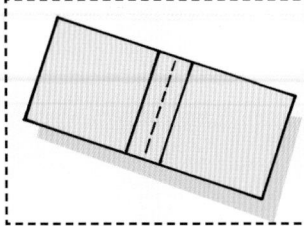

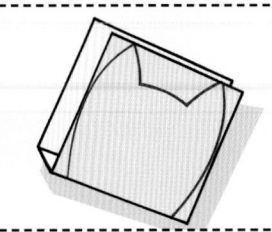

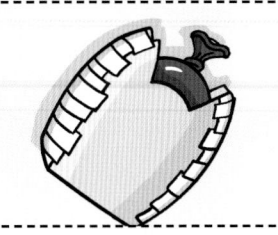

1 Start with a piece of thin card about 20cm x 30cm, perhaps cut from a cereal box. Mark the centre line at 15cm, and then lines 1cm away to left and right. Fold along these two lines to make a base, then unfold.

2 Draw your pal on one face of the card, giving it cute ear shapes. Cut out the shape, and cut the back to match.

3 Lightly tape the sides using strips of paper brushed with glue to make an open box. Insert a balloon and inflate it just enough to make the box bulge slightly so your pal is pleasingly plump.

4 To make sticky-out eyes, cut two eye-sized circles of thin card and two slightly smaller ones of thicker card. Glue the smaller ones onto the bigger ones, then glue the bigger side to your pal.

5 Brush glue onto strips of paper and stick them all over your pal, leaving just the top open. Leave to dry (this may take all night) and then add another layer.

6 When the glue is dry, paint your pal all over with gesso. Then use colourful paint to decorate. Remember to pop the balloon!

Make your glue from flour and water mixed until it is a bit like pouring cream, or use thinned PVA glue.
Prepare this project by tearing your paper into strips about 2cm wide and 5cm long. Tear lots!

17 Recycled boxes

Unwanted bits of scrap paper can still be used to decorate old things to make new things. These boxes can be used to keep lots of little items safe.

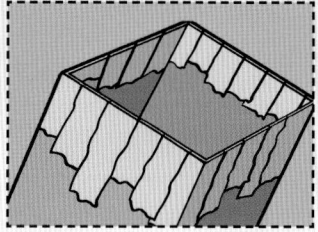  

1 Choose a sturdy cardboard box, or ask a grown-up to help you cut one to the size and shape you want. Glue brown paper over any joins and any cut edges at the top.

2 Tear scrap paper into long strips. A confident rip along the grain of the paper will be straight enough. Glue the strips down the side of the box, mixing light and dark shades to suit.

3 If you wish, ask a grown-up to help you cut a shallow box to make a lid. Cut a hole in the top of the lid so you can "post" your items through. Decorate to match the box.

18 Painted glass

Glass can be recycled, but this uses lots of energy. You can turn your unwanted jars and bottles into new things like vases.

1 Wash and dry your jar thoroughly. Wind strips of masking tape tightly around in bands, twisting the end to give a "bump" so you can easily remove it later. Then brush the jar all over with gesso. When it is dry, add another coat.

2 Next, paint over the gesso with colour. Acrylic paints are the most hardwearing. Let the paint just dry, then unwind the tape slowly to reveal the glass beneath. Make good any bad tears.

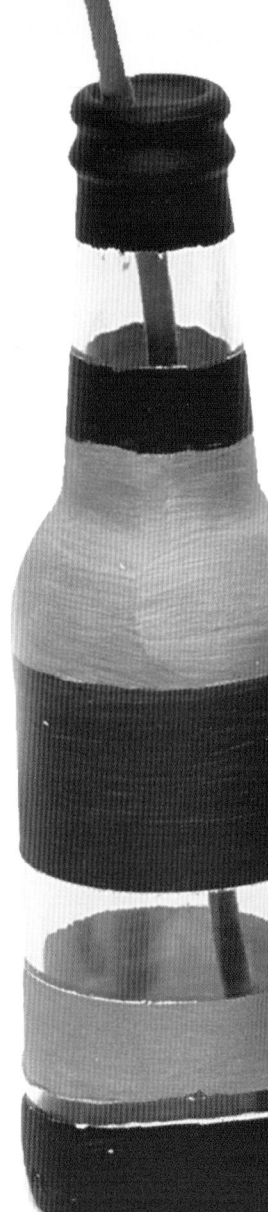

19 Gift boxes

You can also use old pieces of card to make gift boxes in all sorts of colours and sizes.

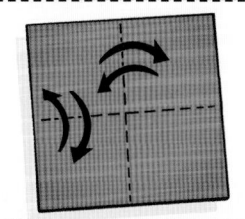

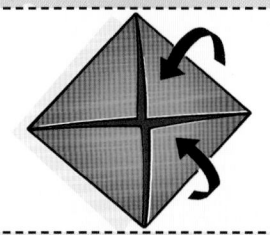

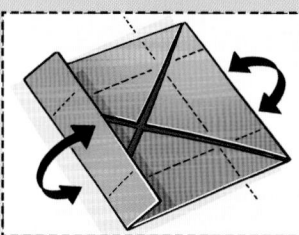

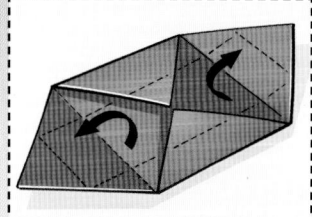

1 Cut two squares of paper, one slightly larger than the other. Take the smaller: fold top to bottom, crease, and unfold; then fold side to side, crease, and unfold. Turn over.

2 Fold the corners to the middle and crease.

3 Now fold two opposite sides to the middle, crease, and unfold. Then fold the other pair of opposite sides, crease, and unfold.

4 Open up two of the corners so your piece looks like this.

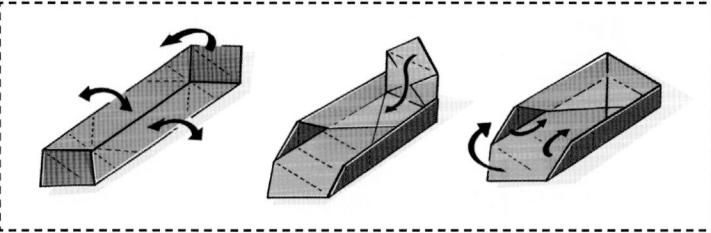

Good-sized squares to start with are 20cm x 20cm and 21cm x 21cm.

5 Now fold up two sides to the middle as shown and follow the sequence shown. As you put the creases in place, the box will come together. Now make a lid from the larger piece.

20 Springtime cards

God promised Noah that there would be summer and winter, springtime and harvest for ever.
   Celebrate spring with these flower cards.

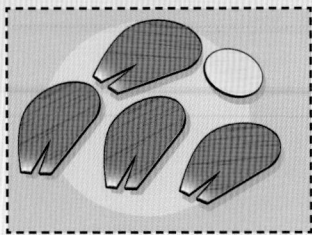

1 Use the template at the back of this book to cut out petal shapes. Cut a thin notch out of each petal, as marked. Cut a coin-sized circle of thin card for the centre.

2 Make the flower. Taking each petal in turn, overlap the two sides of the notch so the petal curls up and tape in place on the wrong side.

3 When all the petals are in place, glue the circle in the centre. Cut out or draw leaves and other details.

21 Carrot boxes

God promised that food would grow every year. Carrots are a vegetable that becomes ready to harvest in the summer.
These quirky gift boxes are a fun shape and easy to make.

1 Take a piece of card 8cm x 30cm. Mark the centre point on each side.

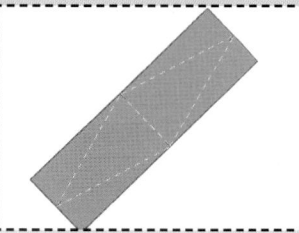

2 Use a ruler to help you mark and crease these lines. Unfold.

3 Punch two holes along the centre line.

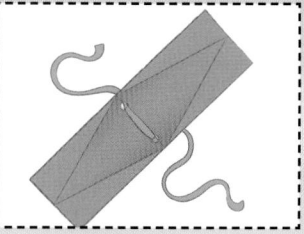

4 Thread through one or more lengths of ribbon. Tie in a bow to look like carrot tops.

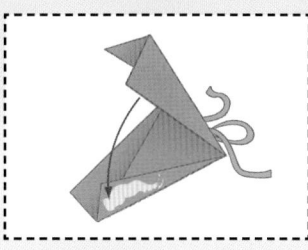

5 Glue the first side shut like this.

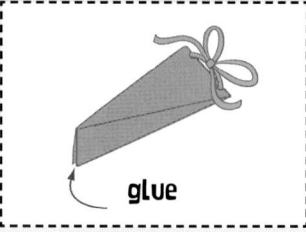

glue

6 Then add your gift before you glue the second side shut.

22 Popcorn

Corn is a crop that can be cooked and eaten in many ways, but popcorn is surely the most fun. This recipe makes one good portion.

1 Put 1 tablespoon sunflower oil, 2 tablespoons sugar, and 1 teaspoon cinnamon into a large microwavable bowl and mix together.

2 Add 20g corn kernels and mix again so that the oil is coating the kernels.

3 Cover the bowl with a microwavable plate and put in the microwave. Heat on full power for 2 minutes or until all the corn has popped – listen out for the pops!

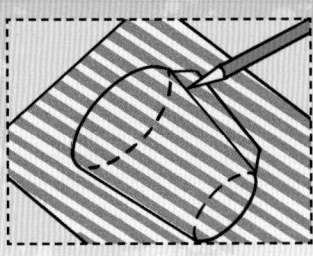

1 To make the pot, use the template at the back of this book and cut out two of these shapes from an old cereal box.

2 Put glue on the flap of both shapes and stick them to the non-flap edge of the other shape.

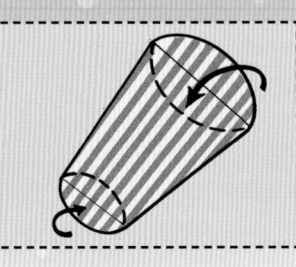

3 Fold in the ends as shown to close the box. If you wrap your popcorn in a cone of greaseproof paper before sticking it in your popcorn pot, you can reuse it at least once.

For spicy popcorn, swap the cinnamon for chilli powder, add ½ teaspoon of salt and pepper, and leave out the sugar.

23 Leaf notebooks

In autumn, the leaves of many trees change colour and fall as the trees prepare for winter. This craft is a clever way to reuse nice bits of paper cut from letters, envelopes, and packaging.

1 Collect pretty leaves in summer or autumn and, if you are not ready to print, press them between unwanted scraps of paper with lots of heavy books on top.

2 When you are ready, protect your printing area with layers of scrap paper or old newspaper. Put paint on a plate. Lightly brush on the underside of a leaf. Lay it paint side up.

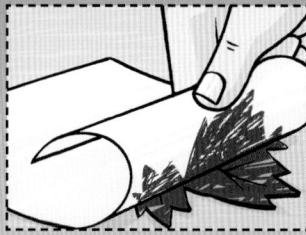

3 Now press a piece of good scrap on the painted leaf: press, lift, and peel. You may get two or three prints from one application of paint, and you can reuse a leaf several times. Print enough for a whole notebook, plus cover pieces on card.

4 When the paint is dry, daw a simple shape around one of your printed leaves. Note where the stalk and leaf tip go. Glue the shape onto card and cut it out, making a snipped V each end to mark the stalk and tip.

5 Draw around the card template on all the leaf prints, using the snipped V to help you position it. Cut out the leaves.

6 Gather your leaves into a notebook, with the plain side up for jotting on. Add the card covers top and bottom. Punch holes by the stalks. Thread one or more lengths of ribbon through the holes and tie as shown.

24 Penguin pals

In winter, the earth becomes colder. Penguins live in cold places all year around, though. Make loads to keep you company in the winter months!

 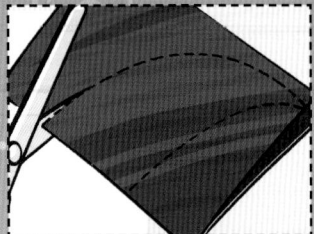  

1 On black card, measure a rectangle 10cm x 20cm and cut it out. Curl into a tube and tape shut.

2 To make the wings, cut a 10cm square of black card and fold it in half. Draw wings as shown, with the fold in the middle, and cut out.

3 Glue wings in place. Draw the belly and eye shapes on white paper and cut them out. Glue in place.

4 On orange or yellow card, draw feet as shown with a thin tab. Crease as shown so you can glue the tab inside the tube and the feet stand flat.

5 Cut a thin orange or yellow triangle for the beak and glue it on. Use marker to add details to the eyes.

25 Heart cards

God sent the flood to make the world good again, and he sent the rainbow to show how much he loved the world.
Make these cards to show people how much you love them.

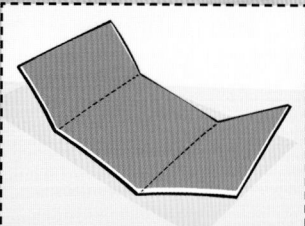

1 Cut out a rectangle of coloured card 8cm x 16cm. Lightly rule a line 4cm from each end as shown. Fold inwards.

2 Cut a square of paper 8cm x 8cm and fold it in half. Use the template at the back of this book as a guide to draw a half a heart shape. Cut out the heart.

3 Unfold this shape and use it to draw two matching hearts from your second choice of card. Decorate if you wish.

4 Glue these two shapes, one on each of the opening edges of the card, so the dip and point are right on the edge.

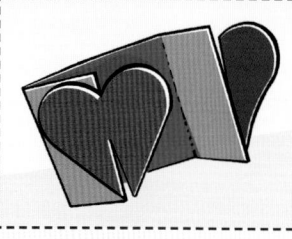

5 Cut two slits down the centre of the hearts to the middle – one from the top down and one from the bottom up.

6 Write your message on the inner panel of the card. Then fold closed and slip the hearts together.

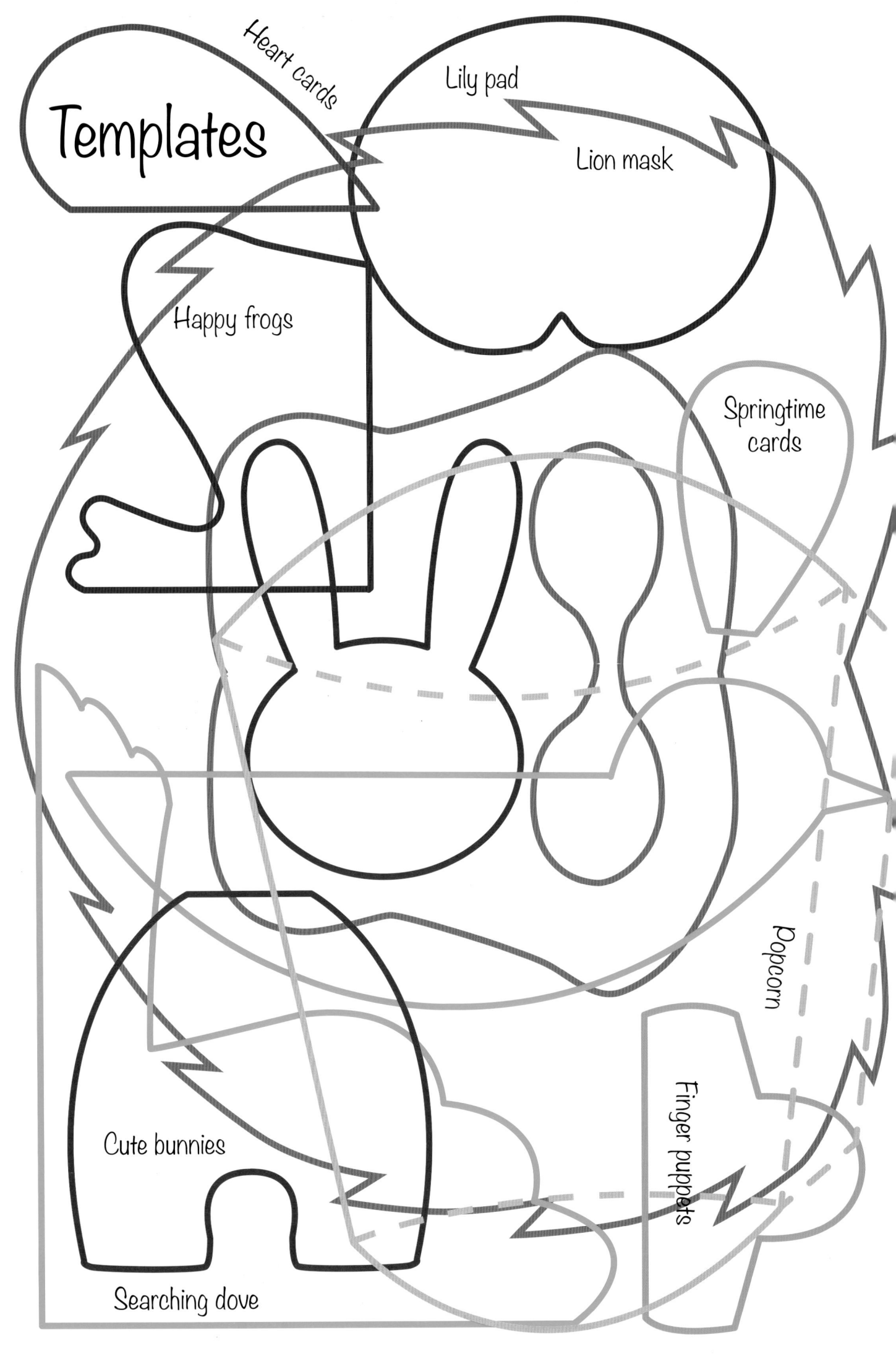

Templates

Heart cards

Lily pad

Lion mask

Happy frogs

Springtime cards

Popcorn

Cute bunnies

Finger puppets

Searching dove